Words like Fire

The Words and Wisdom of Evangelist Reinhard Bonnke

Words Like Fire

The Passion and Wisdom of a Lifetime of Soul Winning. Quotations from Reinhard Bonnke.
© Christ for all Nations, 2008 ISBN 1-9334460-5-6
Published by : Christ for all Nations (USA)
The Ministry of Evangelist Reinhard Bonnke
P. O. Box 590588,
Orlando, Florida, 32859-0588,
United States of America
www.CfaN.org

All quotations © Reinhard Bonnke

All photographs, other than those acknowledged on page 103 taken by Rob Birkbeck
© Christ for all Nations & Rob Birkbeck

Compilation, design & layout Rob & Vanessa Birkbeck

All scripture quotations, unless otherwise indicated, are taken from The New King James Bible.
Copyright © 1982 by Thomas Nelson, Inc. Used by permission. All rights reserved.

Origination, printing and binding by China Printing Corporation, Beijing, China.

Printed in China

Preface

For over twenty years now we have been privileged to have been part of the Christ for all Nations ministry team, working alongside many others in countries around the world and seeing first hand the mighty impact of the Gospel through the power of the Holy Spirit on lives, families, cities and nations.

During this time we have been deeply impacted by the words and wisdom of Evangelist Reinhard Bonnke, his passion for the lost, his integrity and his unshakable and indeed unquenchable love of the Gospel message. Whenever we hear him speak it is always like the first time and we, like others of the CfaN team, make notes of his words that are either said on the spur of the moment over coffee in the crusade technical container, at some press conference or which have become a standard and synonymous with his international ministry.

From a small gathering of just a handful of people in one of our homes, to our CfaN team morning devotions or to an open campaign stage in front of over a million people, his words simplify and present the Gospel message, allowing it to penetrate deep into the hearts and minds of his audience.

We cannot claim ownership to any of the words in this book, it is simply a compilation of a small number of Reinhard Bonnke's quotations alongside our own images of the work of the ministry. This book, through its words and pictures, is aimed at inspiring others to Holy Spirit evangelism either as individuals or in support of Christ for all Nations.

We dedicate this work to Reinhard and Anni Bonnke, Peter and Evangeline van den Berg and all fellow members of the worldwide CfaN team. People from a diversity of backgrounds, nationalities and races yet all part of a single vision—to preach the Gospel message across the length and breadth of the entire continent of Africa and to reach the world with the Good News of Jesus Christ. No words can express the extent of our love, respect and admiration for you all.

Rob & Vanessa

Rob and Vanessa Birkbeck

If you want to catch fish don't cast your net in the bathtub.

Vision

John 21:6
And He said to them, "Cast the net on the right side of the boat, and you will find some."
So they cast, and now they were not able to draw it in because of the multitude of fish.

*On the banks of the mighty river Nile in the shadow of an isolated village,
a lone fisherman casts his net. Juba, Sudan.*

The evangelist is a man with a driving urgency, not a man with two minds. The Gospel and nothing else on earth matters, neither fame, money, popularity or life itself.

1 Corinthians 2:2
For I determined not to know anything among you except Jesus Christ and Him crucified.

Jesus doesn't choose us because of who we are but because of what he makes of us.

Potential

John 15:16
You did not choose Me, but I chose you and appointed you that you should go and bear fruit, and that your fruit should remain, that whatever you ask the Father in My name He may give you.

With her early morning chores completed, young Bola Bola waits for her class to start at the local village school. Made from strips of wood tied together with bark and then plastered over with the mud from ant mounds, the classroom has no windows just holes with wooden shutters.

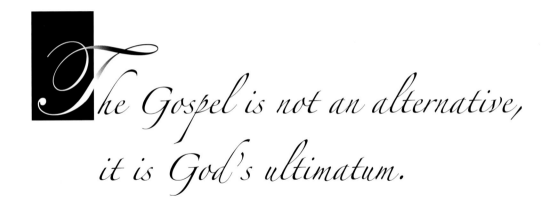

The Gospel is not an alternative, it is God's ultimatum.

imperative

Seemingly oblivious to the huge crowd in the huge crowd around him, a young man finds salvation by accepting Christ. One in the multitude yet unique in God's sight. Ikom, Nigeria.

Faith is a leap into the light, not a step into the darkness.

John 8:12
Then Jesus spoke to them again, saying, "I am
the light of the world. He who follows Me shall not
walk in darkness, but have the light of life."

A sea of hands at the altar call, each one indicating a decision for Christ,
a turn from a life in the darkness to one illuminated by the light of God.

Assurance

I can't purr like a cat when millions are perishing every day. I want to roar like a lion!

Boldness

Acts 4:29-30
Now, Lord, ... grant to Your servants that with all boldness they may speak Your word, by stretching out Your hand to heal, and that signs and wonders may be done through the name of Your holy Servant Jesus."

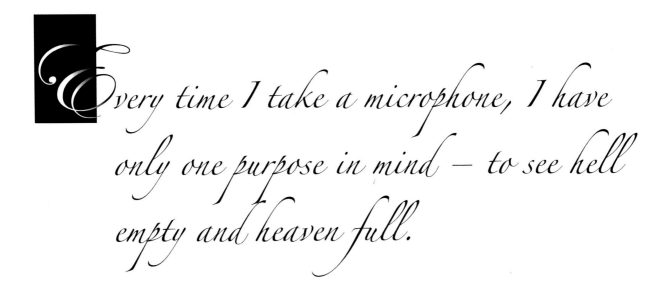

Every time I take a microphone, I have only one purpose in mind — to see hell empty and heaven full.

Romans 1:16
For I am not ashamed of the gospel of Christ, for it is the power of God to salvation for everyone who believes...

On the final day of the Fire Conference, the Church seemed to reverberate as the gathered crowd prayed in new tongues, receiving the all powerful baptism in the Holy Spirit. Belo Horizonte, Brazil.

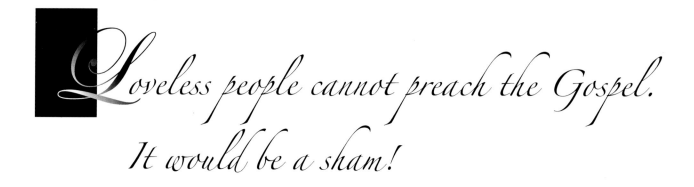

Loveless people cannot preach the Gospel.
It would be a sham!

John 15:13
Greater love has no one than this, than to lay down one's life for his friends.

Sharing the joy of a healing testimony, Bonnke's heart is impassioned to preach the message of salvation to the poor. The miracle of healing delights and enthralls the crowd as they witness the power of the life-changing Gospel message.

A loveless Gospel is a contradiction — a sea without water, sun without light, honey without sweetness, bread without substance... The Gospel is ultimately nothing other than the expression of God's infinite love for us.

John 3:16
For God so loved the world that He gave His only begotten Son, that whoever believes in Him should not perish but have everlasting life.

Yoruba, Masai, Igbo and Hausa... every tribe and every nation, the subject of God's redeeming love through Jesus Christ.

In Christ even the least distinguished people carry kingdom status.

1 Corinthians 1:27
But God has chosen the foolish things of the world to put to shame the wise, and God has chosen the weak things of the world to put to shame the things which are mighty.

The Princess of Calabar timidly waits for the arrival of the evangelist... ambassador and representative of a different kind of Kingdom, armed with a message of love and hope. Calabar, Nigeria.

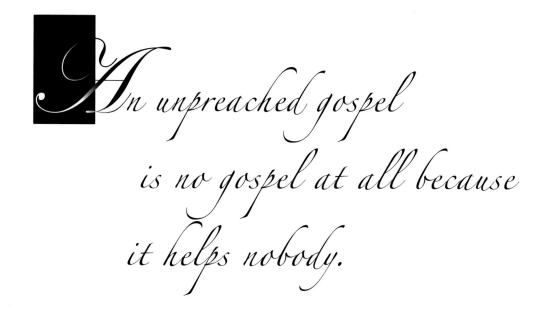

An unpreached gospel is no gospel at all because it helps nobody.

Romans 10:14-15a
How then shall they call on Him in whom they have not believed? And how shall they believe in Him of whom they have not heard? And how shall they hear without a preacher? And how shall they preach unless they are sent?

If you have a hot stove and a cold stove, which one will you use to make a cup of coffee? Get the fire of the Holy Spirit in you, and God 'will' use you automatically.

Acts 2:3
Then there appeared to them divided tongues, as of fire,
and one sat upon each of them.

A kaleidoscope of dazzling colors and warm Christian smiles that reflect grateful thanks as ladies stream out of the morning 'Fire Conference'.

Discovery

It is not the size of your faith but the size of the God you believe in that determines the results.

Perspective

Matthew 19:26
But Jesus looked at them and said to them, "With men this is impossible, but with God all things are possible."

The crusade platform stands seemingly afloat on an ocean of humanity.
Quiet hangs over the crowd as they anxiously take in every spoken word. Abuja, Nigeria.

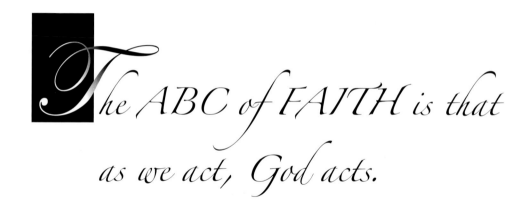

The ABC of FAITH is that as we act, God acts.

Matthew 14:29-33

So He said, "Come." And when Peter had come down out of the boat, he walked on the water to go to Jesus. But when he saw that the wind was boisterous, he was afraid; and beginning to sink he cried out, saying, "Lord, save me!" And immediately Jesus stretched out His hand and caught him, and said to him, "O you of little faith, why did you doubt?" And when they got into the boat, the wind ceased. Then those who were in the boat came and worshiped Him, saying, "Truly You are the Son of God."

On the closing night of every campaign, hundreds of thousands of prayer requests from all over the world in huge boxes are corporately prayed for. All in attendance join their hearts and voices in faith

30

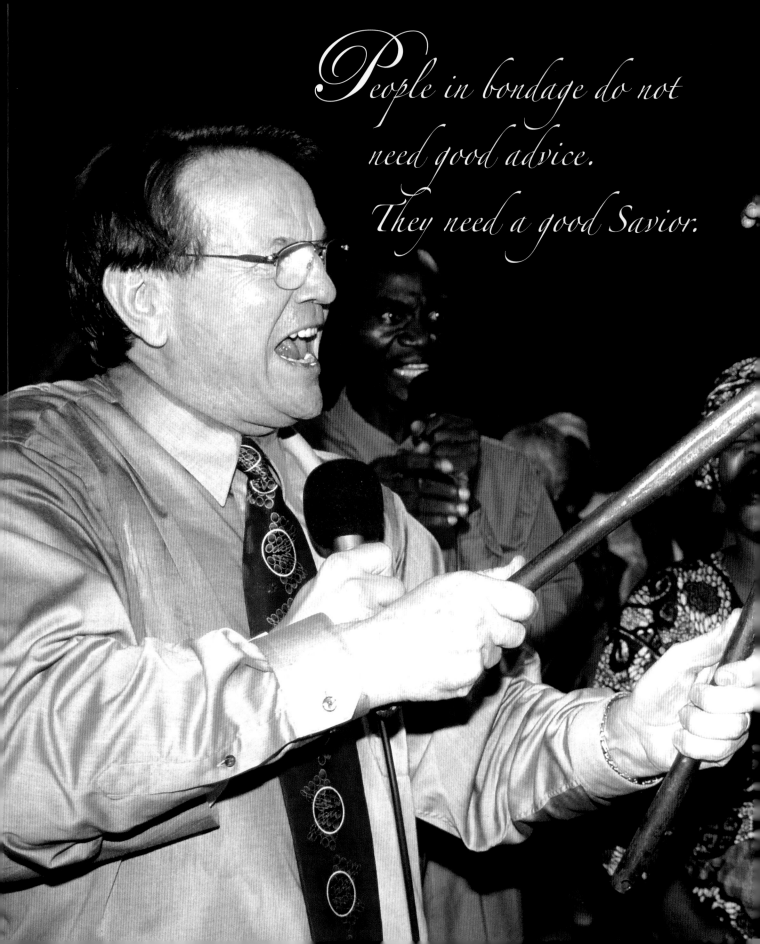

People in bondage do not need good advice. They need a good Savior.

Colossians 1:13
He has delivered us from the power of
darkness and conveyed us into the
kingdom of the Son of His love...

Deliverance

Set free from physical chains and demonic oppression
that have held him captive... released into a new life of
liberty, washed in the Blood of Jesus

The Holy Spirit does not work until the word of God has been spoken.

John 1:4
In Him was life, and the life was the light of men.

After preaching a fiery message at the morning leaders meeting, Evangelist Bonnke goes down amongst the people, laying on hands. (Actual untouched image).

Jesus did not die for Pastors to have well-paid jobs. He died to save the lost.

2 Corinthians 5:14
For the love of Christ compels us, because we judge thus: that if One died for all, then all died...

Densely packed... sometimes as many as eight per square metre, a small section of the crowd that waited for Bonnke to arrive more than an hour in advance. Jos, Nigeria.

*We never do great things
without trying.*

Endeavour

Hebrews 12:1
Therefore we also, since we are surrounded by so great a cloud of witnesses, let us lay aside every weight, and the sin which so easily ensnares us, and let us run with endurance the race that is set before us...

Night after night Bonnke speaks to literally acres and acres of people pressed together to hear the word of God. A crowd so big that it takes hours to disperse.

Discovery

The infectious sound of African rhythm echoes across the expansive crusade ground. Praise is sung to the one whom they have come to worship.

Enablement

John baptized in the cold waters of the River Jordan. Jesus baptizes in a river of liquid fire.

Matthew 3:11
I indeed baptize you with water unto repentance, but He who is coming after me is mightier than I, whose sandals I am not worthy to carry. He will baptize you with the Holy Spirit and fire.

In ancient biblical times the word 'baptism' was used to describe the process by which cloths were dyed. Dyer's hands and the cloth with which they work all take on the character of the dye in which they are immersed. Natural purple indigo dyeing, Lofar Mata, Kano, Nigeria, said to be the oldest in Africa.

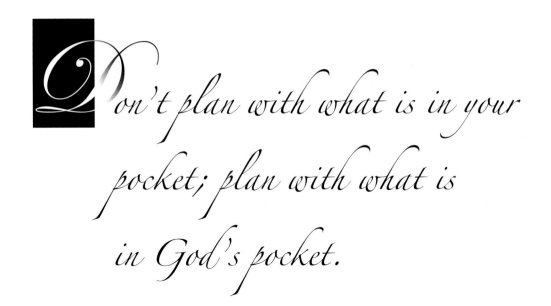

Don't plan with what is in your pocket; plan with what is in God's pocket.

Philippians 4:9
The things which you learned and received and heard and saw in me, these do, and the God of peace will be with you.

On the shoulders of his father, a young boy surveys the amazing extent of the gathered crowd, hoping to catch a glimpse of the one the people call 'Bonnke'.

Go for the purposes of God, and the means to fulfill them will follow.

2 Corinthians 9:8
And God is able to make all grace abound toward you, that you, always having all sufficiency in all things, may have an abundance for every good work.

Every manner of transportation is used to get to the Crusade Meetings. It is not uncommon to see more than four people on a motor bike or 50 people in a pick-up truck all rejoicing and happy to be part of the evening gatherings. Kabba, Nigeria.

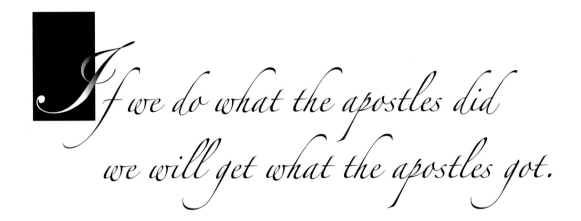

If we do what the apostles did we will get what the apostles got.

Hebrews 13:8
Jesus Christ is the same yesterday, today, and forever.

Mala had put up her hand to receive the greatest miracle, that of salvation, and found that Jesus had also healed her body! Ado Ekiti, Nigeria.

The sun is old and very, very hot
The Bible is old and very, very powerful.

One young man in his teens approached Evangelist Bonnke one day and said that the Bible is too old and has no meaning anymore for the present modern day. Reinhard directed him to look at the sun in the bright morning sky. "Has the sun lost it's power? Does it not shine and shed warmth upon the earth – do we say the sun is cold because it is old?"

1 Peter 1:25a
"But the word of the LORD endures forever".

Night after night thousands of decisions are recorded. Each one an individual indication of a transformed life and a desire to follow Christ.

Enduring

The church that is not saving the lost is lost itself!

Purpose

Acts 2:46-47
So continuing daily with one accord in the temple, and breaking bread from house to house, they ate their food with gladness and simplicity of heart, praising God and having favor with all the people. And the Lord added to the church daily those who were being saved.

The city's largest cathedral is dwarfed by the inmense crowds of people that poured out of the surrounding countryside to hear the evangelist and witness the signs-following gospel. Mbuji-Mayi, Republic of Congo.

Rescue

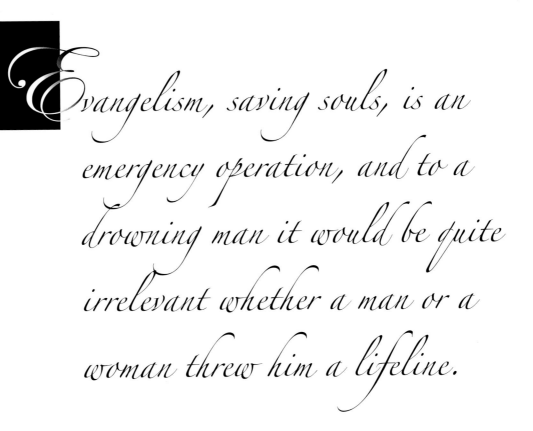

Evangelism, saving souls, is an emergency operation, and to a drowning man it would be quite irrelevant whether a man or a woman threw him a lifeline.

Psalm 144:7
Rescue me and deliver me out of great waters...

A singers voice sounds out across the crowded campaign ground. The Lord is uplifted in praise and worship as His people sing of His majesty and of the wonders that He has done.

Discovery

Motivation

God always works with workers and moves with movers but does not sit with sitters.

Exodus 14:15
And the LORD said to Moses, "Why do you cry to Me?
Tell the children of Israel to go forward.

The truck load of a million 'Now that You are Saved' booklets pulled into the junior school adjacent to the crusade grounds where it had to be offloaded. Without hesitation more than three hundred little heads carried cartons, time after time until the consignment of 5,000 cartons was safely stored, ready for the upcoming campaign. Ikom, Nigeria.

The blood of Jesus is like soap. Soap does not work when it is 'around' you. You have to take it and apply it to yourself. Then you will see what it can do!

Application

1 John 1:9
If we confess our sins, He is faithful and just to forgive us our sins and to cleanse us from all unrighteousness.

I stopped to talk to a group of people who sat under a huge tree outside a local clinic. As we talked, we watched as mothers were taught child care practices including how to bath their babies.

Restoration

The Lord turns broken vessels into vessels of honor.

2 Timothy 2:21
Therefore if anyone cleanses himself from the latter, he will be a vessel for honor, sanctified and useful for the Master, prepared for every good work.

In the main Kabba market, a woman sells her earthenware pots. As she wiped them off and laid them out to show me she saw that one was broken and quickly discarded it. Not so with the Lord! He will take any 'broken vessel' and make it like new!

As fire is to heat,
so Christ is
to Salvation.

Acts 4:12
Nor is there salvation in any other, for there is no other
name under heaven given among men by which we
must be saved.

People rejoice and dance as witchcraft items are burned.
The crowd delight as curses are broken and satanic charms
are thrown into the burning fire. Salvation in Christ brings
separation from demonic oppression.

Salvation

Those eternally seeking the will of God are overrun by those who do the will of God.

James 1:22
But be doers of the word, and not hearers only...

Trucks loaded high with cassava, yams, cocoa, timber and all manner of goods double as passenger vehicles as they ply the routes between cities.

A temporary sound system, borrowed platform, generators and equipment were all hauled over dangerous roads that had just been cleared of land mines to Juba, Sudan where the marvellous message was preached to a capacity crowd. Just emerging from a twenty year long war, the people were hungry for the message of the Gospel.

The great commission must be your great ambition.

Matthew 28:19-20

"Go therefore and make disciples of all the nations, baptizing them in the name of the Father and of the Son and of the Holy Spirit, teaching them to observe all things that I have commanded you; and lo, I am with you always, even to the end of the age." Amen.

The Evangelist's convoy is engulfed by a sea of humanity in Ibadan, Nigeria where over 1.3 Million people amassed to her the Gospel message.

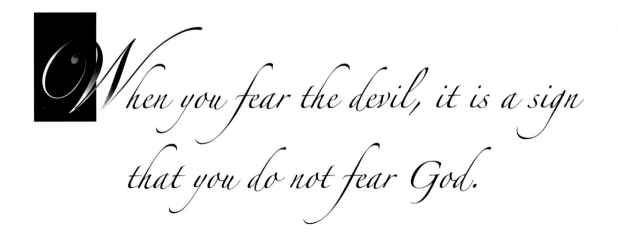

When you fear the devil, it is a sign that you do not fear God.

Ephesians 6:11
Put on the whole armor of God, that you may be able to stand against the wiles of the devil.

As a public demonstration of their new-found life in Christ, all manner of articles of demon worship and witchcraft fetishes are burned while the crowd rejoices. Curses are broken and the people are set free!

Conviction

To know the truth needs no university education.

John 8:32
'And you shall know the truth, and the truth shall make you free'.

As the crowd gathers, children move around the grounds selling all manner of fruit, sweets, bread, water and 'foo-foo' wrapped in banana leaves (a local staple food made from ground cassava).

We are shaped to be an instrument of righteousness in the hand of God.

Ephesians 2:10
For we are His workmanship, created in Christ Jesus for good works, which God prepared beforehand that we should walk in them.

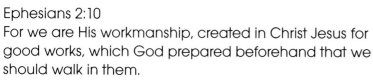
Local musicians lead the crowd in praise and worship. It is a joyous thing when over a million people lift up the name of Jesus as of with one single voice!

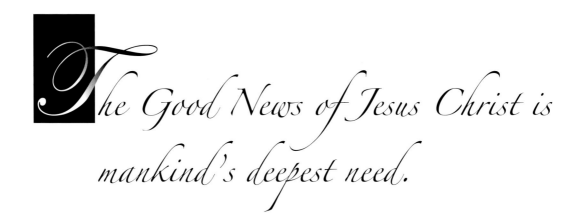

The Good News of Jesus Christ is mankind's deepest need.

John 6:35
And Jesus said to them, "I am the bread of life. He who comes to Me shall never hunger, and he who believes in Me shall never thirst.

Without much in the way of worldly possessions, a young family watch
as a follow-up team come into the village to share the good news of the Gospel
and the great 'riches' of eternal life.

Mercy

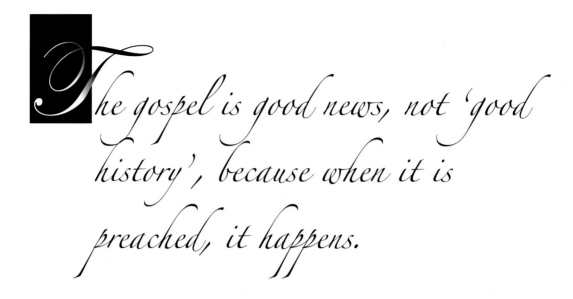

The gospel is good news, not 'good history', because when it is preached, it happens.

Consequence

Acts 5:42
And daily in the temple, and in every house, they ceased not to teach and preach Jesus Christ.

Night after night a huge crowd gathered around the crusade platform, awed by the power of the Gospel, hungry for its life-changing message and eager to listen to and receive the transforming word. Wukari, Nigeria.

Discovery

The pain of poverty can be greater than the pain of sickness.

The Jesus who had compassion on the sick also had compassion on the poor.

Matthew 11:5
The blind see and the lame walk; the lepers are cleansed and the deaf hear; the dead are raised up and the poor have the gospel preached to them.

Bonnke prays for the curse of poverty to be broken, for employment, for good health and for the blessing of prosperity on the city, state and country

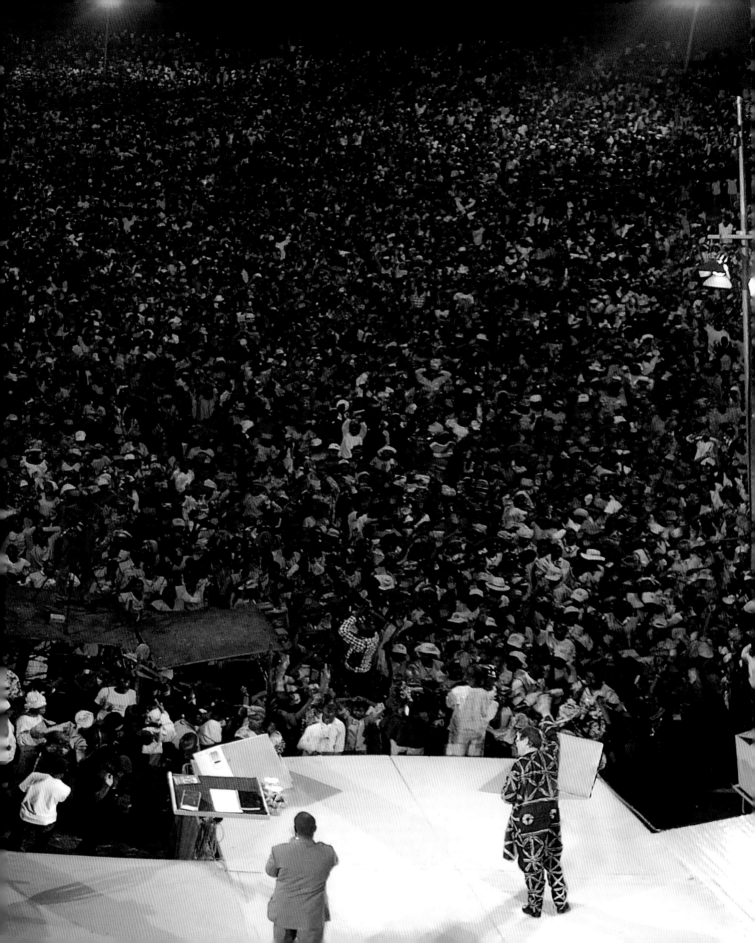

I don't want to play with marbles when God told me to move mountains!

Matthew 17:20
So Jesus said to them, "Because of your unbelief; for assuredly, I say to you, if you have faith as a mustard seed, you will say to this mountain, 'Move from here to there,' and it will move; and nothing will be impossible for you.

In the shadow of the National Assembly Building nearly 100.000 church leaders gather at the Abuja *Fire Conference*.

Romans 12:11
Never be lacking in zeal, but keep your spiritual fervor, serving the Lord.

Church leaders and workers with a heart to be used of the Lord receive the baptism in the Holy Spirit equipping and empowering them for greater things. Oshogbo, Nigeria.

Flies only sit on a cold stove.

Get the fire of God in you, and no demon will come near you!

Zacchaeus spent an hour with Jesus, and the rest of his life giving.

Luke 19:5
And when Jesus came to the place, He looked up into the tree and saw him and said, "Zacchaeus, make haste and come down, for today I must stay at your house."

As the sun sets over the campaign grounds, onlookers seek every vantage point to get a better view of the distant platform. Every housetop is lined with people and every solid branch houses spectators.

The Church of Jesus Christ is a life-boat not a pleasure boat ... all hands are needed on deck for saving the lost.

Matthew 9:37-38
Then He said to His disciples, "The harvest truly is plentiful, but the laborers are few. Therefore pray the Lord of the harvest to send out laborers into His harvest."

An 'army' of counsellors is raised up, each one capable of leading a soul to Christ. Instilled with the heart of an evangelist, these precious workers from churches across the city are equipped to seek out and reach the lost.

When you do business with people you need money. When you do business with God you need faith. Faith is the currency in the Kingdom of God.

Hebrews 11:6
But without faith it is impossible to please Him, for he who comes to God must believe that He is, and that He is a rewarder of those who diligently seek Him.

'Eagle Square', Abuja, the place where Nigerian presidents are sworn in, received its largest attendance ever when one hundred thousand church leaders packed into the closing day of the Fire Conference.

Testimony is given of what Jesus has done! Through faith, bodies are healed, lives are changed and sin is purged.

The wind of the Holy Spirit is not sent to cool us down but to fan the flame!

Power

Acts 2:2
And suddenly there came a sound from heaven, as of a rushing mighty wind, and it filled the whole house where they were sitting.

Church leaders, evangelists and workers all receive the empowering fire of the Holy Spirit. It is an amazing sound to sometimes hear the roar of tens of thousands of people begin to speak in new tongues at one time.

85

Direction

John never called miracles 'miracles' but called them signs, because they were pointing at something.

Luke 11 29:30
And while the crowds were thickly gathered together, He began to say, "This is an evil generation. It seeks a sign, and no sign will be given to it except the sign of Jonah the prophet. For as Jonah became a sign to the Ninevites, so also the Son of Man will be to this generation".

In Juba, Sudan, during each evening of the campaign, the city was literally deserted as almost every single person left to come and hear the wondrous Gospel! After years of bloodshed and warfare, the message of the Prince of Peace was proclaimed.

God has a thousand-year calendar with only one day marked on it. It is marked 'TODAY'.

Urgency

2 Corinthians 6:2
Behold, now is the accepted time; behold, now is the day of salvation.

The huge crowd patiently waited for the conclusion of the salvation message, gripped by its power, unphased by the torrential tropical downpour that thundered over Aba, Nigeria. Bonnke kept going until the closing prayer when one of the sound towers was struck by lightning.

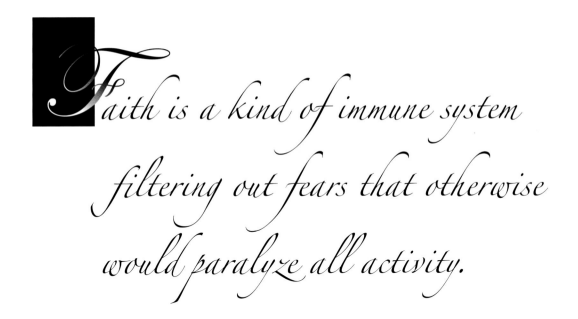

Faith is a kind of immune system filtering out fears that otherwise would paralyze all activity.

Mark 5:36
As soon as Jesus heard the word that was spoken, He said to the ruler of the synagogue, "Do not be afraid; only believe."

In an atmosphere of faith, dozens, sometimes hundreds, push forward to give testimony of their personal healing. Signs and wonders follow the preaching of the word.

A parachute cannot save you unless you reach out and pull the ripcord. The good news about Jesus cannot save you unless you call on His name.

Acts 2:21
... whoever calls on the name of the LORD, shall be saved.

Across the vast expanse of the gathered crowd, each commitment to Christ is individual and unique in God's eyes. An indication of a changed life, washed clean from sin through the wonderful Blood of Jesus.

Perpetual

People are on the potter's wheel of constant change, but the gospel is the eternal word of God to mankind. It is unchangeable! The unchanging Jesus, changes everybody.

Isaiah 64:8
But now, O LORD, You are our Father; We are the clay, and You our potter; And all we are the work of Your hands.

As I sat talking to a group of local pastors little Kemmi (which in Igbo means 'I am fragile') was fascinated by my camera and told me that she wanted to take my photo. I told her that she could but she first had to show me if she had clean hands...

Discovery

I don't want to be a dollar millionaire, but a souls millionaire.

Matthew 6:19-21
"Do not lay up for yourselves treasures on earth, where moth and rust destroy and where thieves break in and steal; but lay up for yourselves treasures in heaven, where neither moth nor rust destroys and where thieves do not break in and steal. For where your treasure is, there your heart will be also".

On a large cleared area on the outskirts of Abuja, Nigeria, hundreds of thousands hear the life-changing and redeeming salvation message.

Hebrews 13:5b
... For He Himself has said, "I will never leave you nor forsake you."

Despite a night of cold rain the central square of Belo Horizonte, Brazil was packed with those wanting to hear the eternal gospel message.

It is foolishness to ask Jesus to come into our presence when He said that He would never leave or forsake us.

Steadfast

The God that went out with the disciples confirming His word by the signs that accompanied it is the same God that goes out with us today... He has never retired.

Mark 16:20
And they went out and preached everywhere, the Lord working with them and confirming the word through the accompanying signs. Amen.

After being born blind, eight year-old Wilfred easily reaches up to snatch Bonnke's white handkerchief. Documentable miracles like this regularly follow the preaching of the word. Ikom, Nigeria.

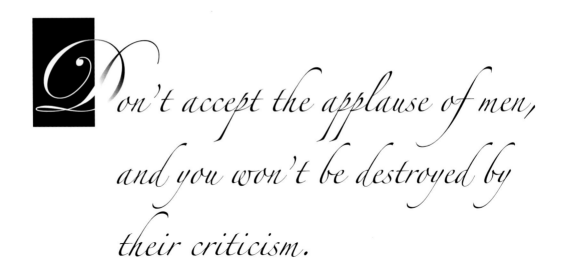

Don't accept the applause of men, and you won't be destroyed by their criticism.

Humility

Galatians 1:10
For do I now persuade men, or God? Or do I seek to please men? For if I still pleased men, I would not be a bondservant of Christ.

Even as the explosive power of a tropical super-cell thunderstorm lashes the crowd, the people remain in an attitude of praise and adoration. Seemingly unaware of the surrounding turmoil and driving rain, they continue to lift up the name of Jesus.

Photographers

Powerful images are vital and essential to communicate the impact that CfaN partners are making through the faithful prayer and financial support. They are also a means by which history in the making has been captured to inspire and challenge coming generations of evangelists to even greater things.

All images in this book were taken by Rob Birkbeck with the exception of those listed below and have been captured on a series of Nikon and Fuji digital cameras.

Vanessa Birkbeck : 9
Oleksandr Volyk : 12, 35, 42, 78
Mark Thesinger : 32
Tom Henschke : 50